AMERICAN C

A History From Beginning to End

BY
HENRY FREEMAN

Copyright © 2016 by Hourly History Limited

All rights reserved.

Table of Contents

Introduction
America in the Antebellum Era
Secession and the First Shots
Early Battles and the Turning Point: April 1861-July 1863
The United States and the Confederacy
Women and Blacks in the War
Military Events, 1863-1865: The War Ends
Reconstruction
The Legacy of the Civil War

Introduction

The American Civil War officially began on April 12, 1861, when Confederate troops fired on the United States' Fort Sumter off the coast of Charleston, South Carolina. Yet like so many times in history when humans have fought each other, the origins of the war stretch back much farther, perhaps even to the arrival of the very first slaves in the English colony of Virginia in the early 1600s. What is more, the full story of the Civil War does not end with General Lee's surrender on April 9, 1865 (and official disbanding of his Army of Northern Virginia three days later); the war's impact was felt for decades afterward, and is arguably still with America today.

Few would question that the Civil War was a pivotal moment in American history, perhaps the young nation's most important to date. As such, each generation of historians has told its story differently, hoping to harness its legacy for a variety of cultural and political ends. The way that Americans have remembered the war is just as important as the war itself, as it shaped future momentous events, including the Great Depression, the Civil Rights Movement, the War on Drugs, and many others.

One perennial topic of debate has been what, exactly, caused Americans to take up arms against each other, and the answer to this question more than any other has changed the most over the decades. While we will explore why successive generations fought about this question and why the truth was subverted, it is important to understand from the outset that the cause of the Civil War was slavery. More specifically, the cause of the Civil War was not primarily the defense of slavery where it existed already, but the protection of the spread of slavery into new and future territories of the United States. Slavery was not only an extremely lucrative form of labor that was beneficial to the enormously profitable style of agriculture in the Deep South, but the internal slave trade was a big business onto itself. After the United States closed the African slave trade and forbade the importation of slaves in 1807, the four million slaves in the country themselves became much more valuable. Their reproductive capabilities were a huge factor in their value and children, too were commodified. Especially in Upper South states like Maryland and Virginia, enslavers literally farmed human beings; they made incredible sums of money by selling their slaves into the cotton kingdom of the Lower South, with Georgia, Alabama, Louisiana, and Mississippi providing some of the most lucrative slave markets. What is more, manumission became completely out of reach for virtually all slaves in America, as they themselves were far too valuable to be dispensed of in such a manner. Thus, even in states where slaves were becoming a less important form of labor, slavery remained profitable and valuable. Other issues on which past historians have placed blame for the war — including states' rights, the tariff, and blundering politicians — would not have been issues at all had it not been for the nature of American slavery.

At the same time that the story of the Civil War includes its causes and its impacts, it is not only about the battles, either. During the war, many other factors played hugely decisive roles its outcome. These included the politics and government of both the United States (commonly referred to as the "Union") and the rebellion, or the Confederacy; the roles of women, immigrants, free blacks, and slaves; as well as cultural and social differences between North and South. All of these factors will be explored herein, and I encourage any reader who finds any particular aspect of this story interesting to explore further; historians have written more books on the Civil War than the number of days that have passed since the war's end. There is much to learn.

Chapter One

America in the Antebellum Era

As previously stated, the complete, complex story of the Civil War should probably begin at least with the landing of the first slaves in what would become the United States. However, for the sake of simplicity and space, we will begin our discussion with the framing of the American Constitution, the document that has shaped American government since its infancy. This document, and the debates that surrounded it, formed the basis of the conflict to come. The issue of slavery was one of the most divisive for the new nation, even before the Constitution was written and ratified. For one thing, the nature of slavery ran contrary to the ideals on which the new nation was built: freedom, equality, and opportunity. In fact, there was a rash of slaveholders who manumitted their slaves in the immediate aftermath of the war. America's "Founding Fathers" grappled with the issue of slavery, and in the end, the Constitution awarded major concessions to the states in which slavery was prominent (slavery was legal in almost all the states at this time), and many of these concessions would haunt American politics until the South finally made good on its promise to secede in 1860. In other words, the divisiveness of slavery did not appear in 1820, or the 1830s, or the 1850s; it was present from the nation's birth. Over ensuing decades, slavery never ceased to be an issue in American politics, especially national politics. While all of the manifestations of the issue cannot possibly be explored herein (nor in a monograph ten times this length or more!), proceed with the knowledge that it continued to play a role in economic, cultural, social, political, and class issues in the nation.

While slavery was an ever-present problem, it flared up at certain points. One issue that the Constitution did not address directly was the spread of slavery. While it allowed for the abolition of the African slave trade, it did not rule on whether slavery should spread as America grew in size, and this question more than any other manifested itself time and again. The nature of American slavery necessitated that it be able to spread, for several reasons. For one thing, slavery was profitable because slaves produced cash crops, which are crops produced in mass quantity for sale at market, often the international market. In the United States these included tobacco, rice, and indigo, but primarily cotton. In order to continue to be profitable, markets must expand. As markets expand, demand for the raw materials — the cash crops — increases. Throughout the antebellum period, cotton especially became more and more profitable. Amazing technological developments in textiles meant that factories in the North and in Great Britain were producing more cheap clothing to meet demand, and hungrily gobbled up more and more cotton. This meant that more cotton needed to be grown in order for Southerners to remain competitive in the global cotton market, and it meant that Southerners needed more land on which to farm. As the United States acquired territory and new states were admitted, it was of absolute economic necessity to Southerners that slavery also be allowed to expand.

Secondly, slavery was an industry onto itself. The trade in human beings was one of the most active and lucrative trades in the country, and accounted for a significant portion of the wealth in the United States. What is more, much of the wealth of slave owners was held in the bodies of slaves, much as your wealth might be in property or stocks instead of cash. If the value of stock that you own decreases, the value of your share of that stock goes down, too. Slaves were an investment; should slavery become less important or less profitable, the humans that slaveholders owned also became less profitable. Thus, any threat to the survival and spread of slavery — real or perceived — was a threat to the wealth of anyone who owned slaves.

The third major reason why the spread of slavery was important to Southerners is directly related to the other two, and deals with the way the American government was set up at the time. While this issue is quite complex, simply put, maintaining a balance between "free states" and "slave states" became vitally important to both sides. The U.S. Congress — The House of Representatives and the Senate — passes legislation, and maintaining the free/slave state balance meant maintaining some semblance of balance in representation between the two factions, so that neither the North nor South could further their own interests on the slavery issue unchecked.

Keeping this balance meant that the slave states could protect the spread of slavery, which meant protecting not only a way of life, but an entire economic system. Most of the major crises that erupted in U.S. politics during the antebellum period revolved around the spread of slavery, and almost every time, the South's leaders either subtly or overtly threatened to secede from the Union — this meant that they would break away from the United States to form their own separate country. It is also important to note that this did not necessarily mean that a civil war would be fought; it was not outside the realm of reality that the remaining U.S. states would simply allow the South to leave without a fight.

One of the earliest of these major crises occurred in 1820, over the admission of Missouri into the Union as a state. Missouri was not clearly Southern or Northern, but its admission as either slave or free would tip the balance in either direction. The debate raged on, becoming more virulent, until a Senator from the state of Kentucky named Henry Clay stepped in. He came up with the Missouri Compromise, which allowed Missouri to be admitted as a slave state, while Maine broke away from Massachusetts and became a free state. What is more, he believed that he solved the territory question by drawing a line straight across the continent and declaring that everything below it was slave territory and above it was free. This system did remain in place for a few decades, but would prove insufficient in the long term.

Over the ensuing decades, the nature of American slavery changed quite a bit. As discussed above, slavery became more valuable as cotton became more lucrative, and slavery as an institution became more deeply entrenched. Fights over the extension and protection of slavery in the halls of Congress were an ever-present problem. Other social and cultural differences also drove the sections apart. The North, especially the cities, was industrializing rapidly. The Industrial Revolution changed the nature of work and daily life for Northerners. The North also saw an enormous influx of immigrants, particularly from the 1840s and on when the Irish potato famine struck. This inflated the population of the North, diversifying its people and creating cultural problems and adaptations that were unique to that section. In other words, the North and the South were looking more and more different as time went on. Although the vast majority of Northerners were not abolitionists — people who favored and fought for the emancipation of slaves — there was a growing anti-slavery sentiment in the North. Some of it was political: especially among Northern Democrats, but increasingly felt by those of all parties, there was growing discontent with the "Slave Power." Some of it, though, was cultural, especially since slavery saw no signs of slowing down or abating, more and more it was becoming a national shame. Most of the world's nations had outlawed slavery: France, Mexico, Great Britain and the British Empire, and several other Latin American and European countries freed their slaves. This humanitarian impulse was growing during the later antebellum era.

The 1850s opened with another major crisis that again involved the spread of slavery. What is often referred to as the "Compromise of 1850" was the passage of a series of bills meant to avoid a secession crisis. Although it is so named, it gave major concessions to the South and helped to fuel the sectionalist fire. The North was especially outraged at the strengthened Fugitive Slave Act, which compelled all people in the nation to help capture runaway or suspected runaway slaves. The decade did not improve sectional relations, which were exacerbated by rising cotton prices. The decision by the Supreme Court in Dred Scott v. Sanford outraged Northerners, who were then compelled to protect slavery everywhere in the United States. The publication of Harriet Beecher Stowe's Uncle Tom's Cabin, as well as slave narratives from escaped slaves like Frederick Douglass and Solomon Northrup, opened Northerners' eyes to the horrors of slavery and fueled anti-slavery sentiment. Crises in the two major political parties also played their part. The Whig Party, which had favored a stronger federal government and maintained a national coalition of Northerners and Southerners, fell apart in the 1850s. In their place, eventually the Republican Party rose, and posed a serious challenge in the presidential election of 1860. This party was more sectional, almost entirely Northern, and some of its leaders openly opposed the spread of slavery (not the existence of it). At the same time, the Democrats were thrown into crisis by the election of 1860; the factions of the party could not come together on a candidate, and ended up running three candidates, which split the Democratic vote and essentially handed victory to the Republican Abraham Lincoln. Southerners believed Lincoln was a direct threat to the institution of slavery, and several states called secession conventions.

Chapter Two

Secession and the First Shots

The immediate cause of secession was the election of Abraham Lincoln, a Republican, to the presidency in 1860, though the conflict between North and South had clearly been building for decades. Abraham Lincoln was actually not President when secession occurred. He was elected in November of 1860, and in the months between his election and inauguration in March 1861, seven states seceded from the Union. South Carolina, which had long advocated for secession, was the first, in December 1860. During January, Mississippi, Georgia, Louisiana, Alabama, and Florida followed suit, and Texas seceded in early February. President Buchanan, who was a Democrat, was in office at the time, and chose not to take action. Rather, he preferred to let his successor handle the crisis, since his election had brought it on anyways. During the time between his election and inauguration, Lincoln was clear that he did not believe that secession was constitutional and planned to take action. It was not clear what that action would be, but most Americans, North and South, suspected war.

Lincoln did not immediately declare war upon taking office. He did not want the North to be seen as the aggressor. What is more, he was determined to treat secession not as an act of a sovereign nation, but as a domestic rebellion: he never acknowledged that the South was an independent country, and truly believed that they were not. He also allowed the South to become the instigator. The state of South Carolina was a hotbed of secessionist fervor and protection of slavery; some of the most ardent supporters of secession and Southern rights throughout the antebellum period hailed from the state. Charleston was a very busy port city in the state, and as such, was an important site of the internal slave trade. It also attracted politicians and politics. The United States had established a fort on a small island off its coast, Fort Sumter. It remained occupied by U.S. troops after secession, and by April, their supplies were dangerously low. The Confederacy warned Lincoln that they considered the fort within their domain, but since he did not acknowledge the legality of secession, he felt it was necessity to resupply the U.S. fort and its men, even though he suspected to be met with hostility. As he attempted to do so, Southern troops fired on the fort on April 12, 1861.

As the artillery battle waged, Charlestonians gathered along the Battery to watch in a very festive atmosphere; not knowing the horror that was to come, they welcomed the opening of hostilities. The troops on Fort Sumter returned fire, but were subdued. They surrendered the following day and were allowed to evacuate. The three casualties of the battle were caused by issues with their own equipment. Nonetheless, this was a momentous occasion: it prompted President Lincoln to call for troops to fight the Confederacy and reunite the Union. Both Northern and Southern men answered the call in droves. What is more, the opening of the war on April 12 and the call for troops on April 15 prompted four more states to hold secession conventions. By May, Virginia, North Carolina, Arkansas, and Tennessee had also seceded. These were not all of the "slave states," though. As more states fell to secession, Lincoln moved to protect those that remained in the Union. Kentucky, Missouri, Maryland, Delaware, and after 1863, West Virginia were called "border states." They occupied both a real and imagined border between the U.S. and the Confederacy: they were slave states that lay between the seceded South and free North, but they also provided a kind of legal buffer-zone between slave and free. All of these states did have to deal with pro-Confederate factions, and there was much violence and guerrilla fighting within them. The divisions within these states reflected how divided the nation itself had become.

Chapter Three

Early Battles and the Turning Point: April 1861-July 1863

There were many, many skirmishes, battles, and engagements during the Civil War. Nearly 300 named battles are recorded, but hundreds of other smaller clashes occurred as well. What is more, all of these engagements were marked by their ferocity and at times, cruelty. There was much anger and hatred on both sides, as each blamed the other for the long-suffering and enormous casualties. Several smaller, less decisive engagements were fought in the few months after the firing on Fort Sumter, but it was not until the summer months that both sides had raised sufficient armies for major battles to occur. The First Battle of Bull Run, or First Battle of Manassas, was fought on July 21, 1861. The North wanted to put down the rebellion quickly, and the surest way to achieve that end was to seize the Confederate capital at Richmond, Virginia. Thus, Union troops headed in that direction. They met the Confederates in Virginia, north of Richmond, close to Washington, D.C. While both sides suffered from poor leadership and were not prepared for battle, it was technically a Confederate victory, as the Union forces were forced to retreat. Although it would be far from the bloodiest battle of the war, it was the bloodiest that Americans had experienced in any war up until that point; it was a sobering experience. Both sides realized that the war was likely to last much longer than they anticipated, and Lincoln called for 500,000 more troops. In many ways, this battle set the somber tone for the war.

The military action of the Civil War is usually separated into the eastern and western theaters. While many of the major battles were fought in the east, fighting was nonetheless ferocious in the west. During the summer of 1861, another major engagement occurred, this time in the west, in August. Missouri, where the Battle of Wilson's Creek was fought, was divided during the war. Although the state never seceded, southern sympathizers waged guerrilla warfare in the south of the state especially, and supported the Confederacy. This battle, another Confederate victory, bolstered Southern spirits and support for the Confederacy in the state.

Several more small or medium sized battles were fought during the remaining months of 1861 and early 1862 in several states and territories in both the east and west. Although none proved decisive in the course or the outcome of the war, they certainly had an impact on leaders' decision making, and the casualties added up. It was not until February, however, that the Union achieved its first major victory at the Battle of Fort Donelson in Tennessee. In the early years of the war, the North suffered from poor leadership: none of their generals or commanders proved themselves capable of winning the war, and leadership of various divisions of the army changed hands several times. At the Battle of Fort Donelson, however, a lower-ranking General named

Ulysses S. Grant caught the attention of Lincoln and his Secretary of War. Over a five-day battle, he managed to capture the Confederate fort on the Cumberland River on the border of Kentucky, an important strategic victory. He also forced an unconditional surrender. This battle helped boost the morale of the Union, which they sorely needed. Over the course of the next several months, they would win more victories, including at the Battle of Pea Ridge in Arkansas, another large battle.

The Battle of Gettysburg (discussed below) is widely regarded as the most important battle of the war, and the battle that turned the tide in favor of the Union. The Battle of Glorieta Pass, fought in March, 1862 in the New Mexico territory, is lesser-known, but nonetheless dubbed the "Gettysburg of the West." While it was certainly less decisive than the actual Battle of Gettysburg, it was probably the most important military event in the far western territory, occurring on March 28, 1862. Confederates hoped to break U.S. control over the territory, and initially, they were successful in forcing the Union troops to retreat. However, they were unable to maintain their supply line, and eventually they too fell back, never to regain that ground again. As the war back east became fiercer, the west became less important, and there was never another engagement in the New Mexico Territory of as much importance as this one.

In the next couple of weeks, two extremely important battles were fought east of the New Mexico territory. The first was the Battle of Shiloh in Tennessee, where the Union forces were again led by General Grant in the western theater, and were again victorious. On the morning of April 6, the Confederate commander of the western theater, General Johnson, launched a surprise attack on General Grant's army, camped on the Tennessee River. Chaos ensued, as Union soldiers scrambled to answer the attack and Confederates scattered in the swamps and heavily forested areas. Johnson himself perished from a gunshot to the leg; when his second in command, General Beauregard, took over, he decided that the troops were too tired from fighting all day to launch a final assault that night. During the night, though, Grant's army was reinforced in large numbers, and this time, he launched the surprise morning attack on the Confederates. The battle was a Union victory, but at great cost. It was the bloodiest battle of the war up to that point: Union casualties numbered over 13,000, Confederates over 10,000. Grant's reputation also suffered, as many in the North blamed him for being unprepared for battle, while U.S. General Sherman, who would later emerge as one of the war's other decisive leaders, won acclaim for his heroism.

Over the course of the rest of the month, the U.S. forces worked to capture the city of New Orleans. The Battle of Fort Jackson and Fort St. Philip greatly weakened Confederate defenses of the city, which finally fell by the beginning of May. This was an enormous victory for the Union, and an even bigger blow to the Confederacy. It cannot be overstated how important New Orleans, located near the mouth of the Mississippi River, was. It was the South's most prosperous city and busiest port. The loss also meant that supplying the army along the Mississippi River would be much, much more difficult. Additionally, the U.S. would not stop here: they continued the offensive throughout Louisiana, and the state would be the first of the Confederacy to fall.

The summer months would see several Confederate victories, however. General "Stonewall" Jackson — so nicknamed for being a "stone wall" against his opponents — won a decisive victory in Winchester, Virginia in May. In June, General Robert E. Lee, commander of the Confederate forces, won a seven-day battle against General McClellan at the Battle of Gaines' Mill in Virginia. Their armies met several more times during the summer, with victories bouncing back and forth, but Lee winning the more decisive engagements. In August, Lee won another key victory at the Second Battle of Bull Run (or Second Battle of Manassas) against General John Pope. Like the first battle on the same grounds outside of Washington, D.C., this win was a huge morale booster for the South and just the opposite for the North. Unlike the first battle, though, casualties were very heavy on both sides, and this battle was considerably bloodier, perhaps representative of the more vicious turn the war had taken in the interim. General Pope was also dismissed from commanding the Union Army of Virginia, one of many changes in command that the Union ranks went through during the war.

The fighting would only get bloodier from here. Had any Americans, Northern or Southern, been told that they had not yet seen the bloodiest days of the war, they probably would not have believed it. Antietam changed that. Fought in Sharpsburg, Maryland on September 17, 1862, this would be the bloodiest day of the entire war (though not the bloodiest battle). What made it more disheartening for both sides was that the Battle of Antietam (or the Battle of Sharpsburg) was not a resounding victory on either side. Lee attempted to make headway into Northern territory by invading Maryland, but McClellan was able to stop his offensive. Lee retreated back to Virginia, but Lincoln was infuriated that McClellan ended the fighting upon Lee's retreat and did not chase Lee's army and deal a decisive blow. Because Lee retreated, it was technically a U.S. victory, though casualties — totaling almost 23,000 — were about equal on both sides. Shortly after the battle, Lincoln took the opportunity to announce his plans for an Emancipation Proclamation.

At no point during the war did fighting cease. Battles continued to rage in Missouri, Florida, Kentucky, Mississippi, Texas, Arkansas, Virginia, North Carolina, and even Indian Territory. The year of 1862 ended with a major Confederate victory at the Battle of Fredericksburg in Fredericksburg, Virginia between December 11 and 15. The fighting took place not only on battlefields, but also throughout the streets of the small town. With General Burnside at the helm, the Union Army of the Potomac launched an offensive on the Confederate stronghold. Sporadic and at times heavy fighting continued for a couple of days. Burnside knew that in order to take the town, he would need to defeat the Confederate stronghold on the heights outside the city, known as Marye's Heights. However, they were heavily fortified, and his attacks failed miserably. He finally retreated after suffering over 12,000 casualties, more than twice the losses on the Confederate side. Southerners were ecstatic at the news, and celebrated over the holiday, many sincerely hoping that the victory was the beginning of the end of the war. The opposite tone prevailed in the North, as both Lincoln and his commanders came under increased scrutiny in the press. The year 1863 would bring much controversy and much perlustration for the president.

The rest of the winter and early spring brought continued bloodshed and battles throughout the country, even in places as far away as present-day Idaho. By late spring, though, a series of decisive battles would be fought, and by midsummer, the tide of war had turned significantly in favor of the North. Certainly, the issuance of the Emancipation Proclamation changed the tone of the war. Several important battles occurred in May of 1863. The first was the Battle of Chancellorsville, a seven-day engagement that began on April 30 and ended May 7 in Virginia, near where the Battle of Fredericksburg took place. General Hooker was now in charge of the Union Army of the Potomac. Hooker was cautious, and this ended up costing him a victory to Lee's Army of Northern Virginia, which was about half the size of his. Lee took a huge chance by splitting his smaller army in two, allowing them to make separate counter-strikes against the U.S. forces. This decision proved genius, and is often cited as proof that Lee was a great general. The battle was not without losses, however; Lee's attacks on the second day of the battle produced huge casualties, and it became the second bloodiest day of the war. Worse yet, Stonewall Jackson was mortally wounded in this battle, which was a huge blow to the South. Not only was he an effective leader, he was a Southern military hero. Nonetheless, the victory was a morale booster for the South, and raised frustrations in the North over military leadership and the course of the war.

While the fighting around Washington, D.C. in Virginia and Maryland was not progressing in Lincoln's favor, two other generals were achieving victories in the west: Grant and Sherman. Grant won several Mississippi battles during early May near the city of Vicksburg, and his siege of the city began on May 18. Vicksburg is located on the Mississippi River and was a crucial supply line for the Confederates, especially after losing New Orleans. The siege finally ended when the city and army, suffering from shortage of food and unable to continue to fight, was forced to surrender to General Grant. They surrendered on July 4 — Independence Day, which marks the signing of the Declaration of Independence. Well into the twentieth century, Vicksburg did not celebrate this American holiday; for them, it was anything but a triumphant moment. At the same time, Port Hudson in Louisiana, also on the Mississippi River, was also under siege. They surrendered just a few days later, on July 9. After the surrender at Vicksburg, Port Hudson was the last Confederate stronghold on the Mississippi. The loss of these two cities was a huge blow to the Confederacy, not only to their morale but also their strategic ability. Northern leaders recognized the huge advantage they now had.

Frequent fighting continued through May and June. As with previous months, victories bounced back and forth, but frustratingly, many of the battles in Virginia especially were inconclusive. The victories in July on the Mississippi River had clearly changed this tone, but not as much as the Battle of Gettysburg, July 1-3, in Gettysburg, Pennsylvania. The meeting of Lee's Army of Northern Virginia and the Union Army of the Potomac, led by General Meade (who took command just a few days before the battle) would be Lee's second and last attempt to invade the North. He and his men were encouraged by their victory at Chancellorsville, and the invasion in Pennsylvania into strictly Northern, free territory (Pennsylvania had never allowed slavery) was meant both to demoralize the North and relieve the fighting in Northern Virginia, which had been long-term and especially fierce. The first day of the battle took place north of the town, where Union forces scrambled to defend their position. Their lack of preparedness forced them to flee through the town and to the south.

On the second day of the battle, the Union and the Confederacy were both better prepared. The Union assembled in a long, curved line, forcing the Confederacy to launch offensives in separate locations. Very heavy fighting with huge casualties occurred on locations like Little Round Top and Devil's Den. On the opposite flank (the left flank), the other half of Lee's Army attacked at

Cemetery Hill and Culp's Hill. Both sides suffered many deaths and injuries, but because they were in a defensive position, the Union was able to hold their lines and ended up victorious. On the final day of the battle, Lee ordered the Confederacy to launch a final offensive on the Union position on Cemetery Ridge. Union troops were positioned at the top of a very steep hill (so steep that the National Park Service has since built a special path so that the top of the hill would actually be accessible to visitors). In what became known as Pickett's Charge (named for one of the three generals who led it), Confederate infantrymen scaled the steep, almost one mile hill as artillery was used to try to weaken Union defenses. However, it was in vain - more than half of the 12,500 men who attempted to breach the hill became casualties, and those who reached the Union army were quickly subdued. The offensive ended Lee's invasion of Pennsylvania, and the defeated men began the journey back to Virginia. The Confederates would never again attempt an invasion of the North.

Chapter Four

The United States and the Confederacy

Other factors besides battles and military actions decided the outcome of the war. Politics played a major role, as did the governments of the two sides. In these regards, the North had major advantages. On an obvious level, the North was not tasked with creating a new government for a new "country" while fighting the war. However, the political problems were much more nuanced than this. The United States of America had been in existence for at least eighty years, and the Constitution had governed the land for most of it. Americans of all kinds — politicians and leaders, civilians, soldiers, immigrants, free blacks — were familiar with the laws of the land, including electoral politics for governing bodies. While certainly vast differences existed between states who remained in the Union, they were at least on the same page when it came to making decisions, levying taxes, choosing officials, et cetera. In other words, there was some level of unity. There was also at least some consistency with leadership as well: Lincoln was able to win re-election in 1864, even after suspending the writ of habeas corpus and making other controversial decisions.

The South, on the other hand, did not have this benefit. There was much quarreling over who should lead and how the government should function. Not all of the states were equally enthusiastic about secession; Virginia needed to be bribed with placing the capital at Richmond to convince her to secede in the first place. The Vice President of the Confederacy, Alexander H. Stephens, spent most of the war at home in Georgia writing letters that attempted to undermine the president, Jefferson Davis. He actually met with Lincoln in February 1865 without Davis's knowledge to discuss a possible peace agreement. While all were united on the issue of protecting slavery, little else engendered the men in the Confederate states to one another; defense of slavery was not quite the same as the ideals of liberty and freedom that had united the Founding Fathers a generation ago. What is more, while certainly some Northerners opposed the war, probably very few opposed the actual existence of the country or expressed great fidelity to the Confederacy. In contrast, Southerners had spent their lives as Americans. Many Southerners owned no slaves, and while the Confederacy was able to cultivate a great deal of loyalty among its population (otherwise, they could not have raised an army), they certainly faced more insubordination and resistance to their very existence than the North. In fact, the U.S. state of West Virginia was formed out of Virginia during the war, since the western portion of the state was so virulently anti-secession and anti-Confederate.

International relations also played a role in the war. Other countries, many of which traded with the United States, were not sure how to react to secession. Would they acknowledge the Confederate States of America as a sovereign nation, or were they merely an American rebellion that the United States was working to put down? Siding with, supporting, or even merely trading with the Confederacy could seriously endanger relations with the U.S. government. At the same time, other countries relied on Southern cotton. No other country felt this pressure more than Great Britain. While today America considers Great Britain an absolute ally, in the mid-nineteenth century, this relationship was not as strong. The United States and Britain fought in the War of 1812 just a few decades ago, and relations remained strained at times. Britain also imported a great deal of Southern cotton for their textile factories. The Confederacy actively courted British support, but in the end, they gained little. For one thing, the U.S. Navy had effectively blockaded Southern ports, so getting cotton out or supplies in was not only risky but also dangerous. Additionally, as the war raged on, cotton production in the South suffered, and Britain discovered that they could supplement the shortage from other parts of the world (including India). What is more, Great Britain had long ago turned its back on slavery. They outlawed the African slave trade early in the century and actively worked against it, and they emancipated all slaves in all their territories in the 1830s. France, whom the South also courted, abolished slavery during their turbulent revolutionary era. As it became clear that the North was also fighting to free the slaves, neither Britain nor France could support the Confederacy and stay true to their ideals. In the end, the South received little support from other nations anywhere in the world, and this had a negative impact on their effectiveness in the war. The South did not have many factories or manufactures, so the lack of imports really hurt them as well.

Geography also played a major role in the impact of the war on the North and South. Most of the fighting took place on Southern soil. The Battle of Gettysburg was fought in Pennsylvania, and a few large battles took place in Maryland (a slave state that did not secede), but otherwise, the South saw much more of the fighting and consequently, a far greater amount of devastation. Damage was done to their infrastructure, such as roads and bridges and railroads, supplies of food dwindled, and there were more civilian casualties and destruction of civilian property than in the North. As the war dragged on, morale sank increasingly lower, and desertions became a problem as Southern soldiers returned home to help and protect their suffering families.

In addition, while the main goals of the war were clear for both sides, how that translated into tactics varied a great deal. As the war dragged on, the North realized that they needed to bring the Confederacy to its knees and prevent it from functioning as a nation. This became especially true after Lincoln issued the Emancipation Proclamation and passed the Thirteenth Amendment; unconditional surrender would be necessary to enforce emancipation in the slave states. The blockade of Southern ports was a major component of total war for the North, as the South was cut off from most international trade. Blocking supply lines, especially railroads, was another. Also, confiscation of property, including food, became another tactic. While the story of General Sherman burning his way through Georgia is largely a myth (in actuality, the Confederates burned their own land and property to prevent it from falling into Union hands), the South saw far more devastation of property than the North, and their daily lives and routines were more disrupted. This is said not to downplay the loss of life in the North, however. Both sides endured terrible loss of life, as well as injury. Men missing arms and legs, or with terrible scars, remained a constant visual reminder of the devastation of the war for decades to come.

The North did not necessarily have all of the advantages. One major disadvantage the North faced was in its military leadership. Lincoln changed command of the Union Army several times throughout the course of the war, due either to insufficient leadership or insubordination on the part of previous commanders. In some ways also, while the North had greater unity among its population, it was not as enthusiastic about the cause of the war as was the South. The South launched a successful campaign to convince non-slaveholders to fight, often painting tithe struggle as as the next American Revolution. While many Northerners desired to preserve the Union out of patriotic duty, or were incensed by the arrogance of the South, others questioned what preserving the Union was worth, especially as the war dragged on and casualties touched more and more lives. Not everyone believed in emancipating the slaves, either. The draft was also an issue of contention, and the class and race issues that surrounded it erupted in New York City in 1863. Infuriated by the new draft laws passed by Congress while also struggling with a diverse population and a still-powerful Democratic party, working-class New Yorkers, among them many Irish immigrants, rioted in protest. These protests quickly turned racial, however: whites began attacking blacks mercilessly, believing them to be the cause of the war, and fearing that emancipation would threaten their own economic livelihood. Lincoln was forced to divert U.S. troops to put the riot down, many of them fresh from the fields of Gettysburg. By the time the riot was ended, more than one hundred people were killed, including eleven lynched African-Americans, hundreds more were injured, and thousands of dollars' worth of damage had been done. The riots revealed deep-seated divisions in the North over the course and outcome of the war.

Chapter Five

Women and Blacks in the War

While the battles have proven endlessly fascinating, it would be a terrible shame to overlook the important roles that women and blacks played in the outcome of the Civil War, just as we needed to pause in the last chapter to explore the differences between the governments and societies of the North and South. The very nature of femininity helped shape the level and kinds of female participation in the war in both regions of the country, and this issue played a role in the war's outcome. Prior to the Civil War, Northern women — particularly middle class, but also upper class women — were active in social movements, and this was socially acceptable. Lower class women were also frequently outside of the home for work. A religious awakening helped bring women into leadership roles, as did advocacy for issues such as temperance (the banning of alcohol). They became active community advocates for social issues and for the poor, and had experience working in groups to enlist awareness, support, manpower, money, and other resources for various causes. This experience became invaluable during the war, when Northern women banded together to support troops and the war effort in a variety of ways. Of critical importance, it was also socially acceptable for women to serve as nurses and tend the wounded or sick. Remember, there was no such thing as antibiotics at this time, and many men died from infections in hospitals or especially disease in the field. The additional labor of women to not only heal the wounded, but cure and prevent sickness by providing good food, cleanliness, awareness, clean supplies, et cetera not only saved lives, it ensured that the U.S. Army was healthier when they went into battle than their foes.

In contrast, women in the South had not participated in such efforts. The social structure of the South was not only complicated, but also extremely rigid. Simply put, women were at all times subordinate to the men in their lives, be they husbands, fathers, or sometimes even sons, cousins, uncles, et cetera. Taking an active role outside of the home was not acceptable for these women. What was more, doing so would not only have disgraced themselves, but these men in their lives as well; the obedience and deference of women was one place from which Southern men derived their status. At the outbreak of the Civil War, Southern women did not have the kind of structures in place that would have allowed them to participate more actively in the war effort, and they did not develop them as the war waged on far longer than anyone anticipated. This was much to the detriment of the Confederacy: not only did it not have the infrastructure or the political unity of the North, it also did not have the kind of social structure needed to support the military.

In addition to women, black Americans played an absolutely crucial role in the outcome of the Civil War. First, they served as soldiers in the North. Whole divisions of black soldiers fought in key battles and bolstered enlistment numbers in the North. While it had been diminishing throughout the antebellum years, there was a free black population in the South that also played a role in the outcome of the war. Many of them, too, served in the U.S. forces, and also worked in other ways to undermine the Confederacy.

Even though they were still held in bondage in the South, slaves, too, had a huge impact on the war, and on Lincoln's decision to issue the Emancipation Proclamation. As they had always attempted to resist slavery, they also tried to resist the Confederacy. This happened especially as word of Lincoln's intention to free the slaves spread, but slaves also recognized long before that point that this war was over their own bondage. As their owners and other white men left to fight, many slaves ran away. Southerners had viciously fought against runaways throughout the antebellum period. Slave patrols prowled the woods and waterways looking for runaways; slave catchers made fortunes returning suspected or actual runaways; and the physical and sometimes psychological retribution visited upon runaway slaves was terrifying. In fact, slave owners were known to sell slaves away from their family and friends, or sell close family members of runaways, such as spouses and children, in order to punish a runaway. The people who worked the Underground Railroad, which was a network of safehouses designed to help guide slaves from bondage in the South to the North or to freedom in Canada, were incredibly brave and noble. However, most slaves realized that the odds of succeeding in running away were slim, and the threat of violence kept them in place.

Thus, when the war broke out, in the absence of many of their former enslavers or would-be captors, slaves took advantage of diminished numbers of whites and attempted to flee the South. This hurt their owners in three major ways: first, they denied their owners of the investment made in their own bodies; second, they denied their owners the fruits of their labors; and third, their absconding was incredibly demoralizing, and even drew men away from the military in order to protect their families and property back home. Black refugees became especially common in areas of close proximity to Union forces. Literally thousands of slaves fled behind "enemy" lines, so many and so frequently that Lincoln and the U.S. government was forced to create policies to deal with them. Historians have long debated the role of the slaves themselves in achieving their freedom. Certainly, the massive numbers of slaves who quit their plantations and fled to Union encampments, most of them willing to fight or work, played a substantial role.

Chapter Six

Military Events, 1863-1865: The War Ends

After the Battle of Gettysburg, Lee and his Army of Northern Virginia had to return home. They had been in very high spirits on the approach: fresh from victory, they were relatively healthy and the weather was more pleasant in late spring and early summer. The retreat proved the opposite: thousands of the men were injured, making movement slow, and they often relied on the healthy for help. Obviously, morale was very low, as everyone understood how significant the loss was. However, bear in mind also that many of the healthy and the sick had been fighting for two years, seeing the carnage and destruction grow worse and worse. Where would it end? The weather was bad on the retreat as well, dampening spirits, and they endured periodic Union raids. When they finally reached the Potomac River at the Virginia border, they found the water level too high to be easily crossed. It seemed there was no relief from the unending misfortune.

The Battle of Gettysburg is often regarded as the turning point in the Civil War, and not just for military reasons. As can be imagined, Southern morale plummeted. Attacking the North had the potential to end the war in their favor, and it failed miserably. The death and destruction were also unparalleled: Gettysburg was easily the bloodiest battle of the war, with around 50,000 casualties, but President Lincoln also played a role in the changed tone with his Gettysburg Address. One of the most famous speeches in American history, it took just over two minutes to deliver at the dedication of the National Cemetery on the battlefield grounds in November. In it, he re-framed the purpose of the war: not only was it a fight to preserve the Union, but it was a fight for the freedom and human rights of all people. It gave the war a much higher purpose at a time when the North needed it, and did just the opposite for the South: they were losing the fight not only for their independence, but also for their very way of life.

Just as it had before, fighting continued throughout several states and territories over the months between Gettysburg and Lincoln's Address. Just days after he delivered it, Grant delivered another major victory to the North by capturing Chattanooga, Tennessee, the last major engagement of 1863. Grant had been given command of the army in the West, and General Sherman helped reinforce them. With this defeat, the Confederate Army of Tennessee was forced to retreat over the border into Georgia. Tennessee was essentially won (though fighting there would continue), and this also meant that the U.S. could begin to wage war in the Deep South. It also made Sherman's March through Georgia possible.

Fierce fighting continued in Tennessee, but in the last weeks of 1863 and early months of 1864, this began to shift southward, with more battles in places like Mississippi and Georgia. In Virginia, General Grant and General Lee fought a series of very famous, very fierce, and very close battles: the Battle of the Wilderness May 5-7, and the Battle of Spotsylvania Court House from May 8-21. Frustratingly for both North and South, both battles were inconclusive, despite huge casualties. Very frequent fighting continued in Virginia throughout the summer, as both sides desperately tried to hold onto towns and push the enemy back. Ultimately, the Union's strategy would prove superior; Lincoln and his advisers knew that the Confederacy could not afford to hold Virginia and protect Georgia, especially Atlanta.

The Atlanta Campaign was in full force by July 1864. Several battles took place around the city, and Confederates desperately tried to hold on. Atlanta was incredibly important: it was one of the few remaining major cities that the Union had not captured, and it was a large railroad depot used to resupply the army. Their efforts were in vain, however; Atlanta fell on September 2, 1864, after the Battle of Jonesborough, and General Sherman continued his march through Georgia, from Atlanta to the sea. It is important to again note, that while Southerners to this day firmly believe that Sherman and his men burned everything in their path, the actual historical record does not bear this out. While some destruction follows any army, the Confederates actually did most of the burning, in order to prevent property from falling into U.S. hands.

Throughout the rest of 1864, the United States won almost every major battle: Opequon and Cedar Creek in Virginia; Westport in Missouri; Franklin and Nashville in Tennessee. Although the Confederacy fought on, and desperately tried to make a comeback, 1865 would open with much the same story: the U.S. continued to defeat the rebellion in more battles in Virginia, North Carolina, South Carolina, Florida, Alabama, and Texas. The Confederacy saw few victories, and won no major battles in 1865 at all. Their troops were exhausted and morale was as low as it could be, and many, who had heard horror stories on the devastation back home, simply left. Finally, on April 9, 1865, General Robert E. Lee's Army of Northern Virginia met General Ulysses Grant and his men in Appomattox. After a relatively brief battle, Lee surrendered, signing documents of surrender that very afternoon at the Appomattox Court House. His army was disbanded just days later, and quickly, the other Confederate armies also surrendered, falling like dominoes. The American Civil War, which no one had anticipated would last so long or cause so much destruction, was finally over.

However, the last casualty of the Civil War had not occurred. Just days after Lee's surrender, Lincoln attended a play at Ford's Theater in Washington D.C. with his wife when John Wilkes Booth, an actor, shot him in the head. There are conflicting reports about what Booth said upon leaping onto the stage after firing the shot, but several witnesses report that he shouted the Virginia state motto ("Sic semper tyrannis"— Latin for "Thus always to tyrants"), or "The South is avenged!" The assassination was part of a conspiracy that also included simultaneous plans to kill Vice President Andrew Johnson and Secretary of State William Seward, though both failed.

Booth died during the manhunt for his capture, while several other conspirators were tried and hung (including one woman). Lincoln himself languished until the following morning, when he passed away. While Booth's attempt to reinvigorate the Southern rebellion failed, he did turn what should have been a triumphant moment for the North into a period of mourning. The war truly ended tragically for all.

Chapter Seven

Reconstruction

The Civil War caused untold destruction, especially to the South. Not only physical destruction, but the unconditional surrender meant acceptance of the Thirteenth Amendment. Slaves were freed and had to be guided out of slavery, allowed to become functional members of the new social order which whites also had to adapt to. States had to not only re-write their constitutions, but also reconstruct their economic systems without slavery. It was a massive, daunting task, all to be taken on by Lincoln's incompetent successor, Andrew Johnson.

The events of Reconstruction can fill (and have filled) volumes. In no way, on no level, was the period easy. First, political problems raged. In the initial phases, the North was infuriated with Johnson's forgiving attitude toward the South, and elected far more left-leaning members of their party, dubbed "Radical Republicans," to Congress. They divided the South into military districts and occupied them, hoping to protect freedmen from angry whites and force emancipation on the unwilling society. Of incredible importance, they passed the Fourteenth and Fifteenth Amendments to the Constitution. While the Thirteenth had freed the slaves, these gave them citizenship, the protections of citizenship, and afforded them the right to vote. For a period of time, the military occupation did fulfill its promises; freedmen enjoyed access to services and opportunities, voted, and even served their government at the local, state, and national levels. The House of Representatives even went to far as to impeach President Johnson, though the Articles of Impeachment were not approved by the Senate and he was not removed from office.

While civil rights did improve during these years of "Radical Reconstruction," no victory was without a price, and white Southerners fought hard. As more states ratified new Constitutions, rejoined the Union, and sent representatives to Congress, they worked to exercise political power against Reconstruction, regaining the right to vote and mobilizing to fill politics with old Southern loyalists. At home, the Ku Klux Klan and other similar terrorist organizations were formed to frighten blacks away from the polls, away from whites, and away from action. They issued violent threats and visited unspeakable retribution on those who did not respond accordingly, including widespread torture and murder of individuals and their families.

As the South fought on in these ways, the North grew weary. They had been at war with their own countrymen since 1861, and by the mid-1870s, they were ready to be done. Additionally, new, more pressing issues were drawing their attention, including the rise of big business, the arrival of new immigrants, and increasing labor unrest. Northerners were more concerned about divisions between classes of Americans rather than sections, and thus were willing to capitulate to the Compromise of 1877: in the contested presidential election of 1876,

Republican Rutherford B. Hayes became the victor. In exchange, he and the Republicans agreed to withdraw troops from the South, ending the period of Reconstruction. In the years that followed, Southerners would use political, legal, and violent methods to reduce the black population to a state of virtual slavery. While their fathers had fought and died in the divisive war to free the slaves, the sons made blacks the sacrificial lambs of national reunion.

Chapter Eight

The Legacy of the Civil War

Though the war ended in 1865, and Reconstruction ended in 1877, the legacy of the war lived on for generations, and is arguably still a factor today. Civil War memory is a rich historical subject, which we will only briefly touch on here. Many scholars have explored how the South and North reunited, allowing old enemies to once again become fellow countrymen. One powerful way was through how the country remembered and commemorated the Civil War. The war itself, as well as the antebellum periods, were romanticized, even mythologized. Americans began to think of the "Old South" as a gentle place with a stately way of life, ignoring the fact that much of what they waxed nostalgic for was literally built on the backs of millions of enslaved human beings. By ignoring and even working to undo the memory of slavery, Americans were able to whitewash the war, erasing its most bitter, most embarrassing, and more destructive aspects. Northerners and Southerners came together on the battlefields upon which they fought to erect monuments, and later generations still gather to reenact battles or visit the sites, without a second thought to the true cause and ultimate failure of the war.

After the end of Reconstruction, Southern whites, particularly those who had been powerful before the war, worked to regain their power and again subordinate the freedmen. For the sake of reunion, and out of their own racism, the rest of the country allowed it to happen. Southerners used several tactics to do this, not the least of which being terrorism, but also including mass incarceration, sharecropping and debt peonage, denial of access to any sufficient public services including education, and legalized segregation (called Jim Crow laws). The South was not alone in exercise of racial discrimination; at best the North stood by and allowed Southerners to exercise this kind of domination, and at worst, they, too participated in it. In fact, during the Great Depression in the 1930s, President Franklin D. Roosevelt was only able to pass some of his famous New Deal legislation by appealing to Southern Democrats by blocking African Americans from access to any of the programs.

Racial discrimination continued to be virulent well into the twentieth century, throughout the country. Finally, conflict erupted during the Civil Rights Movement, which lasted from the 1950s-1960s. It was anything but static, taking on different forms and different tactics, as well as different leadership throughout the period. Poignantly, in 1965, at the 100th anniversary of the end of the Civil War, President Lyndon B. Johnson signed the Civil Rights Act into law, a key piece of legislation that purported to fulfill many of the failed promises of Reconstruction. The previous year, the Voting Rights Act would finally deliver the rights supposedly guaranteed in the Fifteenth Amendment.

Issues of race continued to impact the United States throughout the rest of the twentieth century and into the twenty-first. In the 1970s, riots erupted over forced integration of schools in Northern cities, especially Boston. Epidemics of poverty, drug abuse, mass incarceration, violence, even the AIDS virus continue to impact the black community much more than the white, and especially recent historians have shown how these issues are rooted in the legacy of slavery and discrimination. While it is no longer acceptable in most places to express the kind of open hostility toward African Americans that was the norm into the 1950s and beyond, recent events like the Rodney King riots in the 1990s, attacks on President Obama's birth certificate, the shootings of unarmed black men by police officers, and the resulting Black Lives Matter movement, remind us that despite the loss of life in the Civil War, the legacy of slavery lives on.

Printed in Great Britain
by Amazon